Winds of C

Hear The Truth

See The Illusion

Know The Prophecy

Claire Guichard

First Published
November 2021

Dedication

To my husband Paul for his unwavering support for this book writing thing, for his input and for all the listening of my accounts over the years, even at the time they are been given by spirit.

To all of our children, and most importantly my grandchildren, they are the most important, they are our future.

I want them to live as they believe.

To the world of Spirit, because I wouldn't have written this book if they hadn't have given me the information.

Quote

Belief is Everything

When you believe in something you know it to be true for
you

All that you are believes in the certainty of your truth

And that is everything to you

The choice is yours

Claire Guichard

Foreword

Before I knew Claire, I would have described myself as a skeptical person with regard to the spiritual realm. This altered when I met Claire. Before we become a couple, I awoke one night with the overwhelming feeling that my maternal Grandmother, whom I had been very close to as a child, was sitting on my bedroom chair and telling me that Claire was the right person for me. Needless to say, we became a couple almost twenty-four years ago and from that day I have pretty much hung on to Claire's journey deep into the spiritual heart of this world.

I say THIS world because I have become increasingly aware that spirit resides not in some separate plane or dimension far away but coexisting with us as we make our way through our lives. I have found myself becoming ideally positioned as a witness to Claire's visions, dreams and experiences over the years and have tried to pick up some valuable knowledge of how to "see" the signs and messages spirit give us whilst on this eventful ride.

For Claire, I see these interactions as having become a way of life; for me a constant reminder that we have senses beyond the five we learn about at school. There has even been the odd occasion when we have both received the same message independently and have verified its reality. Way beyond my ability though, I witness both night and day, the names, places, events that Claire receives from spirit. These often come in a dream state for her or sometimes more wakefully, but often as I see it when the mind is literally on the right wavelength. She will tell me she has received a name or an event, which we will then follow up with some research. Increasingly this has seemed to lead to a linked series of revelations and premonitions, some of which Claire has now recorded in this work.

My role as a witness to these events is important to me because I am often uniquely placed to see the way which Claire has been guided to the events and people in this book and so act as the critic. But along the way I have also become accustomed to "seeing" the energy which some nights completely block out the light from the window or feeling her heart race or seeing the look change on her face in day time events when she knows "someone" is there to tell her something.

Paul Guichard

Contents

Chapter One

The Beginning

'Claire...You must remember this it is very important!'

The words were as clear to me as if a living human being was stood next to me and had spoken yet the person speaking to me was not from this realm, place or time, he was from the spiritual world, and he was here to give me a message and to make sure that I didn't forget!

I am yet to understand why I have been chosen with this information, but what I do know is that I must pass it out to as many people as possible. My heart centre tells me this is so, there is no time to procrastinate about whether I should or shouldn't, it is required to be written and it needs to be now. I have spent the last few years since receiving these dreams, visions, and signs to ignore it any longer.

I feel that my spirituality has always been inside me; as a child I used to have a recurring dream, in it I was moving along a tunnel, the sides seemed like they were revolving, flashing past faster and faster and there were greens and reds with a circle of white light at the end. I could feel myself getting closer to the light, and I would start to panic as I got closer, and I always woke up just before I reached the end crying. I don't remember telling my mum about it, and yet it kept happening. Eventually, they did diminish, as I grew older, but I never knew what it was about. It is only now I have more of an understanding.

As children my dad used to take me and my younger sister out into the countryside. He showed us how to suck the nectar from the nettle flowers, how to use a blade of grass to whistle with, we used to giggle trying to do it, he told us that if we felt we were not safe; we could do this and someone would find us. Bramble picking, samphire picking too were other things he would do with us he taught us the natural ways of seeking plants and foods out.

I always remember he would talk to me about local ghost stories, and how he had encountered them on his travels.

The Green Lady from Thorpe Hall was one of them, well known in the area and often seen walking the gardens. A love story gone wrong, a woman still hoping to see her lost love. There is a tale of a young man thrown from his horse that he rode along the A18, in Lincolnshire his gravestone is in the dyke close to where he was originally buried, a reminder of a life lost, but seen on occasion by drivers.

It seemed that my dad was preparing us, there was times when my dad would take us to see this gentleman in a small cottage which overlooked the church, whilst there we would play a card game called 'memory' it required you to match two cards, by remembering where they were. I think back now clearly it was a game of intuition. I recall my dad would ask how we had got on.

As a teenager I always used to sit on our metal garden gate, we lived in a council house, but on that gate, I would think, I would people watch, I would wonder where the people passing by lived, were they married, where did they work, so many stories from watching.

At eighteen I saw a deck of Tarot cards advertised on the television; I had no idea what they were but was drawn to buying them. I kept them in a yellow silk scarf and used to practice with them.

I didn't know anyone who read Tarot cards, no one in my family did that I knew of, yet I was always intrigued with a local lady who used to walk around the town I lived and grew up in.

She was a few years older than me, she always dressed in black. If I recall correctly there were rumours that she was to be feared. Yet I never felt that instead I wanted to talk to her but never did.

I also remember buying myself an apron in my late teens, I didn't really understand what it meant but it resonated with me. It said on the front the following words of how I recall them;

I Think Therefore I am

But if I only Think

How do I know I'm Thinking

I Think

I Think

I Think

Which I have since come to know was Cogito, ergo sum, a philosophical statement by Rene Descartes translated it means 'I think therefore I am' (Wikipedia)

It appears that even as a teenager, somehow my inner self was trying to get my attention.

In those days there wasn't any internet, whereas today so many learnings are available online. When I was a teenager, the internet was barely been used by the public, I remember Amstrad coming out and a family member buying one. Was I interested in it, not particularly, seemed like hard work at the time... Oh, how times change!

I experienced the first passing of a family member at age three. My mum was expecting her sixth child.

I remember been squeezed tight into the corner of the winding stairwell as my mum was brought down the stairs by two ambulance men, this memory has always been with me, it's one of those that stay the in the recesses of your mind, I am sure we all experience them. As they drew level with me, and I can imagine how fearful I would have looked, a three year old child seeing her mummy been taken away, and her mummy being in so much pain.

The second ambulance man said to me as he drew level with me 'it's alright ducky, we will take good care of her' and with that, they were gone.

My baby sister never came home, her name was Benita

I have been told by my mum that I was the only one of the children that kept asking where the baby was. My mum never knew where she was buried as she was still in the hospital recovering as she nearly died herself. It wasn't until much later, years later that our Daddy found out where she was buried to be able to give my mum some closure.

When I look back there were several deaths within the immediate family, my Grandad when I was around eight who unfortunately committed suicide.

When I was eleven, my maternal Nanna passed, she had cancer. I remember us all going to see her for a party, and we knew it was to be the last time that we would see her alive, as she was getting sicker by the day.

We always had pets as I was growing up and we lost several pets over the years, I had a rabbit that was scared to death by the Jack Russell that lived next door. I was devastated. We took in a stray cat and called her Suki, she was a beautiful tortoiseshell but she was hit by a car, my mum told me not to go look at her before we buried her, but I did, it wasn't pretty without going into details. I have always been more of a cat person. Strangely many years later when I was training with my own mediumship my mentor mentioned the name 'Suki'. It was good to know she remembered me.

At eighteen my paternal Grandmother passed, she sat in her chair and said, 'I've had enough' and passed away. When I was twenty-four, my paternal grandfather passed, around three months later my dad passed away from a heart attack. I was twenty-four and four months pregnant at the time with my first child.

In some way, all these happenings allowed me to experience death at a young age, were they learnings for me I wasn't sure then, but undoubtedly, they were. I came to know what death was, and I knew it happened to everybody at some time in their life. In some ways, it appears I was always destined to walk this path.

Chapter Two

Twenty-Twenty

Since the beginning of the year 2020, the world has been in a catastrophic period. There has been a pandemic raging, where a 'coronavirus' had somehow taken over our lives, and created so much unhealthy vibrations for everyone. It was called 'Covid-19'

We are still living with restrictions more than a year later, although who is to say what will happen in the future, yet my experiences in some ways have shown me!

We have had lockdowns, where we had to stay at home, only able to go out for essentials and exercise. A lot of places had to close, shops, pubs, gyms and much more. I was put into a furlough scheme due to the closure of the charity shops I was working in and sent home.

The strange thing was I never felt in fear, I don't know why I didn't; it just didn't make sense to me. I was the same person I had always been from not knowing about it, to hearing about it.

There were initially different versions of how the virus came into being, which quickly became a pandemic, an emergency that infiltrated across the world.

I remember though been at work just before the first lockdown started, and the fact someone had received a flu shot meant they got sent home. Why is that? I asked myself. Were they more at risk? For me there wasn't any logic and I was baffled.

What I am going to talk about in this book is the information I have received from the spiritual realm and how it connects to this world issue, where I have been led to different people, which led to more discoveries that I didn't know about.

Who am I you might ask; I am a person much like you that has been chosen by people in the spirit world to receive what I feel is significant information in regards to the past year's events. I don't know why I was chosen, and I very much doubt I am the only one, in fact there are a lot of people that have spoken since this all began and I sincerely hope that more people talk about their experiences.

If I was going to believe anyone, I would rather put my trust in the spirit realm than the physical world we live in.

Why you might ask?

I think they can see what is happening, they have been aware of it coming. There are already people they connect with to pass information to. Everything they have given me has astounded me.

I have no reason to not trust the spiritual world, when I was on a course in January of 2020, the tutor said to me after a trance speaking, he said 'you fully trust spirit don't you?' At the time I shrugged my shoulders and smiled, but I do.

I work in a spiritual capacity giving readings, guidance and spiritual healing to people, I love this work, there is a need for it, and I think that need will become more prevalent over the months and years to come, so many people will lose their way. Everything that they believed to be true will be questioned and they will search for answers.

I have always been connected in some way to something that is so much more than most of us realise is out there for us.

It doesn't make me any more special than you or an authority on certain subjects, but I firmly believe that the information received does play a part and I have to make it available to you.

So, I ask you to read my experiences with an open mind, and then ask yourself does this cause any doubt in your mind to the narrative that has been told, take note of how your body reacts, how your senses perceive the writings, does your instinct kick in, like it does when you meet someone and get an instant dislike for them, or the good feeling you get when you connect with someone and you make eye contact, you instantly feel a recognition with them.

I am not writing this book to change your mind, as we all have that free will and choice, and we each have our belief systems and perceptions.

For some people, though it might just get them thinking about this whole situation, and when one starts to conduct their own research, you discover so much more.

As for my own spirituality, my connection to the spirit world, the divine, the consciousness, the source, whatever people perceive it as, it is there to guide me, to help me, and it has strengthened in ways that I hadn't envisaged in the eighteen months since before the pandemic started.

All I will say is I have seen too much, heard too much, felt too much in the way of experiences, dreams, visions, signs to know that there is more than most of us know, and I would love for as many people as possible to find this part of themselves, it is all within you, if only you were prepared to search for it.

I wrote the following article recently in January 2021, I often wake with a title in my mind, and Illusion came to me at some point last year, and it wasn't until January 2021 that I woke with the urge to finish it, and so I did. I sent it to a friend to publish on their website, and he replied instantly saying brilliant, the next morning it was published.

Illusion

An interesting word don't you think.

Let me start with a definition;

 noun. something that deceives by producing a false or misleading impression of reality. the state or condition of being deceived; misapprehension. an instance of being deceived. ... a perception, as of visual stimuli (optical illusion), that represents what is perceived in a way different from the way it is in reality. (Dictionary.com)

Is there a lesson to be learnt from really taking in what this meaning is trying to say?

As a whole are we being deceived by a false or misleading impression of our reality? Every day we may come across an illusion, something we thought was true and honest but was found to be not so. Only discovered when the illusion was broken. You could take the example of a relationship, where you believed it to be happy, loving and so on, and then that illusion was shattered when the other person ended it for no reason and you didn't see it happening.

A creation of circumstance and thought of how our mind leads us to believe something, can you think of a time when this happened to you?

For me for the above a feeling of Déjà vu, of being in a place what I didn't know, but yet I recognised! One would be a visit to Lindisfarne on Holy Island, which is off the coast of Northumberland. My husband and I parked up; I jumped out of the car and felt such excitement and was eager to set off. I told my husband how I was feeling, and just knew I had been there before.

Even now typing this I can feel the excitement and the energy of that moment. It might not always be a positive feeling though, and the illusion we see and our thoughts surrounding it may have a negative connotation.

How many times in our lifetimes are we led to believe that illusions are real? 100's, 1,000's, take a moment to think on this question, ask yourself was it for your best interests or not?

The following excerpt is from Joe Brewer's article 'How Political Mind Control Works' but take the politics out of it, please.

*"This is how our minds work. We construct **illusions of meaning** that we then act out as meaningful things while we go about our lives."*

So, are we living under one mass illusion, one that has been created for us? How do you feel about that? Is your life impacted by not fully grasping what is real and what is an illusion?

This is just me musing because so many people now are struggling to get through their daily lives, due to so many external concerns that aren't of their own doing.

Why do we allow ourselves to fall victims to illusions, is it because they are enticing, do they give us hope, do they give us despair, I don't think there is one set answer as the amazing beings we are, for each one of us our perceptions will be different. What we believe our reality is will be just that, and some will be too afraid to rock the boat as they say, and others will have none of it and will move forward and challenge.

We have a journey to undertake each one of us, I would urge you all to trust yourself first and foremost, to understand that you as a unique individual you have the power to understand what you need to be happy and fulfilled and whatever else you desire, and for some of us, a helping hand may be needed to start you on that journey.

Remember that even though we are individual people, we are all connected by our energies. In essence an invisible thread that unites us all, just imagine if those threads were as strong as they could be, the incredible power that would have.

"There 'maketh' the strands of life you will overcome when you stand together"

Chapter Three

When Did It Start?

Dreams have always been a big part of my life, so weird and wonderful and foretelling too. I fully believe our dreams happen for a reason, they can appear as guidance to help us in our everyday lives, or as in my case, they can sometimes foretell the future.

One of those times was when I was walking down a corridor with a red stripe on the floor, and at the end was someone waving at me, but I didn't know who it was. Not long after I phoned a neighbour who is a friend of mine to see if she was alright, her husband told me she was in the hospital and said I should go visit. Which I did, as I walked along the corridor there was a red stripe on the floor, I saw my friend at the end waving to me. She was so pleased to see me. Yet I knew I had been given the information to find her.

Another vision was seeing a heart monitor that quickly went to critical. I was sat watching it happen.

Not long after I was visiting a family member in hospital, and a patient in a bed directly opposite, went into what appeared to be a crisis, the monitor was bleeping, Dr's and nurses ran into the ward, very quickly pulled the curtains around, again a premonition of something that happened not long after.

There has also been a couple of dreams that my husband and I experienced within the same night, not only that we shared the same dream. In the first one I was in the middle of a war zone, there was men in camouflage running all over the place, there were military tanks, blasts going off. I thought to myself as I am not as interested in the war stories like my husband is, so I told them to go to my husband who was fast asleep next to me. It wasn't until a couple of days later my husband said to me, I had a strange dream about a man in the forces, and the information he gave him was that his death wasn't as it was reported, he was a Captain. I also remember asking my mentor at the time as it felt very important to us. It was suggested we light a candle for this gentleman and say some words for him, which we did, may he rest in peace.

The second one was also to do with the military, again my husband and I had coinciding dreams. I was in a house and I had a young son, my husband was also there. I was stood at the door which was at the side of the property looking outside, I saw an aeroplane which was camouflaged, and it was heading towards the house. I shouted to my husband to come and look. It quickly banked skimming over the top of our house. In my husband's dream I pointed the plane out to him and he came and stood next to me. What he saw next as he looked through the window was the plane crash land but where there should of being houses there were none. The plane he saw crash though was a plain light colour.

As I usually do, I did some research, and I also put a social media post on our local group, as we do actually live on an old RAF base. I had several replies and managed to get to speak to the local historian. As soon as we started chatting, he said;

'I know exactly which plane you are talking about'

I had explained that I was a clairvoyant and medium, and he understood as had also had experiences himself. With his knowledge we came to know that this aircraft was likely to have been a Vickers Wellington MK II which crashed into the married quarters houses close to where we used to live on the 22nd October 1941.

Where we used to live our row of houses was parallel to the row that was demolished by the crash. Even today you can see the difference in the houses as they were rebuilt as some point.

The crew as follows;

Sgt J K Millar, Sgt G L McInerny, Sgt L W Rogers, P F Tracey, Sgt M R Forty and Sgt Taylor, all these men except for Sgt Taylor died in the crash. They were nearly home returning from Bremen and were trying to land back at the base.

Rest in Peace to these men, and our condolences to the families of these men.

For years I was always told you need to write your dreams down, and I'll admit I didn't not until I received a visit which I realised was much more than just about me and my life. When I receive information, I often awaken first and then I receive it in that in-between state of being awake and asleep. Yet this isn't always the case.

This dream visitation happened in July 2016, and to be honest, it was so random and nonsensical I thought well what I am supposed to get from that. All I heard in a half-waking state was the following;

'Claire you are going to have a dream, and you need to listen carefully as it will be very important

There was no time frame, nothing to tell me what it was about, or when I would have the dream, but I did make a note of it.

In the mornings I would always speak to my husband about my dreams, and as time went on, he was often with me when information was received and can corroborate my story. I had various other dreams which I believe pertained to me and my journey, some of which I talk about in this book.

September 2017

In this dream there was a man in it called Pesus, possibly Perseus, I say this because sometimes the spiritual world does not speak so clearly, although this could be my hearing too. He was looking after a woman, who appeared to have lost her mind. There were swords in the water, one of them belonged to Perseus, which was retrieved while the others were left in the water. The body of water was a rectangular pool, in a square; there were buildings around the perimeter. The ground was dusty and stony. He had lived in disguise and was a very powerful man; he fought others to protect the woman, he saw me and beckoned me to him and told me to sit next to him.

I laid my head on him and there were two others that I felt were gods. I felt that I was protected by them.

Was this dream relevant, to my mind it is due to me been protected by these gods, they didn't want harm to come to me. I felt that I was an Oracle in that time.

May 2018

In front of me were a pair of hospital doors, they had round windows on them. I was floating above the ground and was very quickly been propelled forward towards the doors, they started to open. I didn't want to go through them and stopped myself, and promptly woke. I stopped myself because it was really bright the other side, and I took me back to the recurring dream I had a as a child.

In **July 2018**, in my dream, I was stood outside my house and a mother chimpanzee was carrying her baby she was walking past my house. I reached out to say hello to the baby and he grabbed my fingers, his mummy stopped and looked at me. She then turned around and came back to the gate at the entrance to my house. She then passed me her baby to hold; as she did, she was looking at some symbols on my door. She told me they represented the Sun, the Moon, the Sea and the Stars. I turned to look at my door but I couldn't see the symbols.

I was still stood holding her baby, when I looked back at her she had changed appearance from the chimpanzee into a woman she wore a cream coloured dress, with brown beads around her neck, and a brown sash around her middle, she had brown hair. What was the reason for her to give me her baby? Had she entrusted her baby to me for protection, or was it protection for me, she then turned and walked away in the direction from which she came.

I wondered initially when I started this book and was going through my dreams whether this had anything to do with the current circumstances, but then I saw a post that mentioned chimpanzee adenovirus. So, it got me thinking did this dream have anything to do with the chimpanzee adenovirus.

The answer is possibly.

Then I also found upon reading the Bible, the following in regard to the Sun, the Moon and the Stars and Sea, the symbols that were on my door.

Two signs in the entire bible called 'great signs' found in Revelation 12 1-2 and Revelation 15 1, that Jesus said there would be signs in the sun, moon and stars, and the vision of an astronomical sign in Revelation 12 1-2 is the only sign that simultaneously contains all three.

'There will be signs in the sun, moon and stars, on the earth nations will be in anguish and perplexity at the roaring and tossing of the sea' Revelation 12 1-2

There is also a passage that says 'a woman clothed with sun, with the moon under her feet, and a crown of twelve stars on her head. She was pregnant and cried out in pain as she was about to give birth' Revelation 15 1

Did the chimpanzee woman who saw these symbols on my door know something I wasn't aware of? The clothing she wore suggested a very spiritual woman, and appeared to be looking for someone, was she looking for me?

I have never been what you would call religious, although as a child, I enjoyed Sunday School, I never liked having a red dot in the attendance book if I wasn't able to attend. I always enjoyed the visits to church whilst at school., and when it came to choosing options the school really wanted me to do Religious Education, but I didn't see what they saw clearly. Also, when I was a teenager, I used to think about nuns and their lives and thought about what it would be like to be one. Even now I enjoy visiting churches if we are on holiday, and the time we visited Paris, the well-known Sacre Coeur drew me instantly. Unfortunately, I never got to go inside, hopefully, one day I can return.

I have seen a nun several times whilst at home, one particular morning my husband had gone to work, and I went back to sleep, I woke and saw a Nun walking into our bedroom, carrying a very neat pile of laundry. She said hello to me, I was so surprised, but I said hello back as she carried on her way. I feel I have connections to religious life in previous lives.

I have also woken and seen a nun at the side of my bed, with her hands together as in prayer, looking over me.

This takes me back to a dream where I was told about a convent that used to be in York. I was given the name of St Joseph's. I researched for one of that name, and eventually came across The Monastery of St Joseph, it closed in 2013 as it had become unmanageable for the few nuns that were still residing there. At its peak in the 1940's there were forty nuns living there. They were 'The Poor Clare Colettine Nuns' It is also interesting to mention that a connection on social media, said to me that I have to mention St Francis of Assisi to you, he was an Italian, a catholic friar, deacon, a mystic and a preacher, he also founded 'The Poor Clare's Order'

I went with my daughter to a mind, body and spirit event and whilst there the was a retailer was selling rosary's, I picked one up all I remember was they were black in colour, my hand started shaking fairly violently and I had to put them down quickly. It had shocked me with the depth of feeling. My own energy clearly recognised them; I definitely feel I have lived in religious orders.

There was also a time I woke suddenly, and as I opened my eyes, I thought to myself, it's very bright in here yet it was the middle of the night! I then heard in my mind 'Claire turn over' and then again 'Claire turn over' to be honest I got a bit scared because I didn't know who it was. Now I wish I had!

2nd October 2018

I could see in front of me a table, and on the table was a magic book. I had my hand held above the book with my palm downwards. I tried to raise the book from the table, and to my surprise it moved, I pulled my hand away quickly and it dropped back down. Someone who was there told me to try again, so I did, and it rose quicker than the first time. I then woke up. I didn't know who the voice belonged to.

I felt from this that my power, my energy was building very quickly. I was able to master tasks without much practice.

The next dream visitation arrived in **October 2018**, to be exact the **6th October 2018**.

I saw three suns in the sky, they were huge, there were also mountains in the background, and I heard these words spoken

'a place where there is three suns'

I was slightly baffled and still half asleep as I was starting to drift off again, then I was shouted at and was told

'Claire you must remember this, it is very important'

I always sleep on the right-hand side of the bed, and when I looked to my right, I saw a uniformed man stood next to my bed, I could distinctly see he had three stripes on his arm sleeve. A Sergeant I understand, he did not give me his name. The fact I was told that it was very important, connected it for me to be related to the first dream in 2016.

Whenever I receive information, I always like to do an internet search to see what I can discover, because I believe there must be a reason for receiving these messages. So, the next morning this is exactly what I did, I entered into the search bar 'three suns in the sky and the first item that came up was about the 'sun dogs' phenomenon in China.

A sun dog is when an optical illusion is created due to the atmosphere, it is also called a parhelion in meteorology.

It is because of the light being scattered from ice crystals in the clouds. What it shows is the sun in the centre, and a sun either side so in effect it looks like three suns!

Well, I came across another website and on it where there were lots of accounts from other people that had dreamt about three suns in the sky.

I did leave my comment about my experience as follows;

October 10, 2018 at 9:23 AM

I had this dream/visitation on the 6th October 2018...I was seeing three suns, they seemed huge, 'a place where there are three suns' I heard, I was a bit baffled, and half woke and saw a military uniform next to me, only the sleeves and his stripes at least three, and I heard 'Claire you must remember this'

So, it appeared I wasn't the only one who had received information similar to what I had been given.

The question would be why are so many people having a dream that is very similar but all having three suns in them? What is the significance, were all these people receiving a premonition, a prophecy?

I didn't know the answers to these questions, but as time went on it became clearer.

10th October 2018

I visited a wellbeing event and went to listen to a talk, within it, we did a meditation. Whilst in that meditation, I was in a forest and came across a cottage, I knocked on the door and a woman answered the door, she asked me inside, and she gave me her name 'Agatha Wilson'. I mentioned it to a friend who told me that this was the name of a character in the well-known books 'A Discovery of Witches. Agatha Wilson was a demon in the story.

The stories are about vampires, demons and witches. It wasn't a story I had heard of prior to this, I was intrigued to say the least.

Unbeknown to me the TV Series of the same name was released on the 4th September 2018, approximately four weeks before my dream. I have wondered what the correlation may be in relation to this book, I think it could be in respect of myself learning more about my abilities, as the lead lady was about to find out about her gifts, but also the fact that we just don't know who may live alongside us in our everyday lives.

Demons! Witches! Vampires!

We have all heard the stories haven't we Count Dracula, The Pendle Witches, Werewolves for instance. Stories that have long been in our history, it is interesting to mention that also within these books are time travel, where the main characters go back in time to search for a book.

Yet what 'A Discovery of Witches' is about ultimately is Love between two different factions a vampire and a witch. For me this is the crux because love is powerful, there is strength in love, and people will die for love.

What people also need to understand that love in the spiritual sense not just the physical it is absolute, because when you love true self, and accept your true self you become more powerful than you realise and this is where we need to be as a whole.

We are all part of one consciousness, we are connected energetically, and when you come to know this, you understand so much more and yet there are some people that do not want us to discover this about ourselves they require you to be oblivious.

Why do they require you to be oblivious you might ask, well my thoughts are that by doing this they keep themselves safe? They don't want people to know that there is more to us as humans, that there is a part of us that can allows us to expand our minds, our consciousness so we too can interact with our higher self, the power within, our soul, and with others, but not in the conventional sense.

When your heart centre opens, the amount of love you feel being expressed is unlike anything you have felt before. Love is energy, it is vibrant, it is powerful, it is the only thing that will give us mere humans a voice, a purpose, the knowledge to trust and believe that we are so much more than we ever thought we were. With that we are free.

November 2018

I woke to find myself in shallow water, the water was clear, I could see grasses and trees in what appeared to be a tropical forest, I looked around and could see my husband and one or two others that were with us. We started to look around, I stopped to look into some water that appeared deeper, in it I saw what looked like a gateway and on each pillar were horse's heads, my husband had walked a bit further and was stood on the edge of a massive circular structure, I shouted to him 'stop! Don't go any further' it didn't feel safe. I walked up and stood beside him looking down into this circular abyss. My feelings on this were it was to do with the City of Atlantis. Very interesting.

I did do some research around this, watched some videos on possible locations of Atlantis, but for me if those horses' heads on a gateway are found, you will find the mystical city.

December 2018

In this dream I was rudely awoken by my alarm going off, I had woken earlier and had fell back to sleep. In the dream I was at a well-known psychic development college, here in the United Kingdom. There was my husband, my tutor and another man. All of the other students had gone out, we fell asleep and I woke up but there were snakes everywhere, I was trying to extricate myself from the room but also trying very hard not to step on them, and to stay calm! I'm not too fond of snakes if I am honest!

The tutor then shouted and said there was someone on the telephone for me, I went to the table and picked up the receiver, it was an old-fashioned black telephone with a dial. The very well-spoken English gentleman on the other end said to me;

'Claire are you there?' to which I replied 'yes' he then continued and asked if had seen his German collie...

I had the strongest feeling that I was talking to Sir Arthur Conan Doyle. Upon doing some research the next day, I did find some information with a photo of him with his collie, and the fact that he had gone missing.

Several years ago, the children and I went to town to do some Christmas shopping, always a fun experience buying gifts for loved ones, but when there are four it could get to be a mammoth task. We were in a book store, and the children were looking for something for their dad, and I saw this book right on the top shelf, it was the Arthur Conan Doyle's 'A Life in Letters' I reached up to get it and showed my daughter, saying 'I think your dad would like this' and she said no. We carried on around the shop, and when we got to the place where it was it wasn't where I had left it, it was on the floor at my feet! I made the decision to buy the book as a gift for my husband from his daughter.

Imagine my surprise upon waking one morning and I would say around two years after it had come into our home, with a tremendous urge to read it!

My husband never did read the book, it was clearly meant for me, hence the connection I feel I have with him.

28th February 2019

I went up, up, up into the sky, through a hole, I was on a hill, and saw a man with his back to me, he held a staff in his left hand and was looking at the view in front of him. I walked up beside him and looked at him. He turned to look at me, yet he did not speak. I felt very humbled in his presence. He was dressed in a cream coloured dress, with a brown sash, reminiscent of the lady and the baby chimpanzee. Again, a very spiritual encounter. I was sweating from this experience when I woke up, so much so I didn't get back to sleep.

When my husband woke, I said to him 'I know this is going to sound weird, but I think I met God last night' I will say that everyone's perception of 'God' will be different, and that's perfectly ok, this man was what I would perceive as God, yet it was the profoundness of his presence, I am not sure why he didn't speak to me or why I didn't ask any questions. I knew it was important though.

31st May 2019

I was living in my previous home, and a bus came through the back door into my living room, it kept trying to reverse out and was scraping my wallpaper off! Eventually it got out, and I went outside to talk to the driver about the damage, but upon returning I tripped over a seal and as I went into the house, I saw this huge giant snake, it then saw me! I shut the door quickly and it slithered up to the door, it started banging its huge head on the glass trying to get to me, I ran, should I go outside or upstairs I thought to myself. I quickly chose to leave the house as I would be trapped upstairs, so I left by the front door and escaped. I was pulled out of the dream and was left feeling dizzy.

This dream in effect was a catalyst to my awakening as such, even though I had followed my path for some time, this experience seemed to up the ante and I felt that things were speeding up, and I should stop running from myself. Obviously as time went on it would become clearer that I had a job to do.

21st June 2019

I was awoken in the night and closed my eyes, at this point I saw writing appear, the word I saw was 'chocolate' and a sensed a man looking at me, he felt like a doctor. I will say here that Sir Arthur Conan Doyle was a doctor. I knew from eating chocolate that it didn't sit well with me, so I felt this was a definite message to give it up!

5th October 2019

In this dream, I went to a venue to set up for a wellbeing event where I would be offering readings to people. I had set up my table and left the room for a few minutes, I returned to find everything was packed up and the event was not going to take place. There was a woman, a nurse she said to me 'it can't happen because the patients have to come this way.

I wondered what she was talking about, what patients? And why would they be coming to events venues? They are hardly hospitals are they!

I have attended events at the Newark showground in Nottinghamshire and Lincoln showground in Lincolnshire, both venues later came to be used as Coronavirus Vaccination Centres, hence them having patients and attending events venues.

I had to laugh at the absurdity recently of attending an event now they have been allowed to happen again, and how the wellbeing market was in one building and the other side of the car park was a 'Vaccination Centre' They couldn't be more different if they tried.

There were staffs from the vaccination centre, coming across peering through the windows to see what was going on, I even saw one-person venture into the venue and walk around looking at all the exhibitors. Ironic!

This same night as sometimes happens my dream flicked to a different one. At the time I was going to a local writer's group and in the dream were a couple of people I knew from the group. There was also a woman I didn't know sat opposite me with grey eyes. She spoke to me and said 'awaken doll' I opened my eyes in the dream and they were like a silver glittery kaleidoscope, it felt like it was me, but it wasn't. I couldn't see in front of me and was putting my hands out to feel, and one of the women from the writers group held my hands. I did get a picture of an Edwardian desk though, a writer's desk! I then woke up.

This was the culmination of my awakening I feel. The desk, the writing all leading to a path I hadn't envisaged.

January 2020

At the beginning of the year, I decided I needed to go to a well known psychic college, the course I booked was three weeks later. It was a healing course, and was great, yet I experienced something that made me feel very angry at the time, and a lot of people that know me would say they have never seen me angry! I may get annoyed at times, but I'm not an angry person.

In the mornings there were lectures to attend if you wanted to, I think it was the Thursday morning. I walked into the room and took a seat next to a friend I had met whilst there, and we waited for it to start.

The lecturer said to someone behind me 'are you ready to go?' and this person said 'yes, it has just got very interesting' I thought it an odd thing to say, as I had just walked into the room and I was late, and not many other people were coming in at that point.

The first thing we did was a meditation, for those that don't know it's a breathing exercise that with practice can allow you to reach an altered state within your mind, creating a place of calm. It all started off well, but the deeper we went, I began to feel uneasy, this is why! In my mind I felt that spirits were trying to invade my mind, they were at the perimeter and were trying to get in, the only way I can describe this was that on cartoons where you get ghoul shapes floating around this is what they looked like to me. I cannot express how angry this made me feel because what right did someone have to attempt to do that to me. It was like they were trying to get into my mind but why?

We got to the end of the meditation, and I knew this feeling had come from behind me, and I looked around to see the person who said 'it just got very interesting' still in a meditative state, yet I could feel the energy waves receding back to them, strong and powerful. No-one else seemed to be affected. It was surreal to say the least.

My friend asked if I was, ok? I said no not really and explained. This was the reason I had to go on this course, a lesson within a lesson.

Chapter Four

David

Fast forward to the **13th March 2020**, I had a very realistic dream of visiting a man, I had the strongest feeling that I had to go visit him so I did, it didn't seem to matter that I had no idea who he was. I jumped in my car and set off to see him alone. Time then jumped in my dream as I found myself sat in a living room, this man was sat in an armchair and I was sat perched on the edge of a sofa with floral covers it was in front of a window. I had my notebook and pen in my hands. I couldn't make out his face because the sun was shining on him. I sat there and explained that I felt I had to come and see him and that I knew he had a lot to teach me. I also felt that he was a very spiritual person and interested in the paranormal dark side if you like, and he was also a known person. This sort of freaked me out a little but I was intrigued.

Suddenly the dream then changed and what I saw was the man I had been visiting in the sky with a silver cord attached to his midriff, there was another man with him whom I didn't know either, he also had a cord attached to him. The cords were connected to the earth plane. They both held swords and were looking downwards and thrashing their swords. I looked down and saw two other men with swords, they were trying to sever the cords of these two men in the sky. I wondered why? What was the reason? I did feel that the men on the ground were trying to stop them from going higher. Or becoming more noticed? I had the feeling it was a fight between good and evil.

This dream was very realistic to me, and when I woke up in the morning, I recounted it to my husband Paul. Then suddenly I said 'Oh and another thing, he lives 250 miles away and it's to the South and not the North' We have lived on the East Coast for all of my life, I was born and raised in Louth, Lincolnshire, a place of outstanding natural beauty.

I didn't know how I knew this I just did, but as a clairvoyant, clear knowing is a part of what I do. What I do know is that it was a clear message that I had to discover who this person was, and boy was I in for a surprise.

Please take note that this dream happened before the first lockdown which started on the 24th March 2020. I remember been at work on the 23rd March.

17th April 2020

I was awoken and could see energy all around me; upon closing my eyes I saw the name *'David'* very clearly in a beautiful script font, I often see writing in energy, it usually shows to me in green. I had no idea who this was, I didn't know anyone called David, and there wasn't anyone in the family called David. I asked a couple of friends if it could be connected to them, but it wasn't.

The world of spirit can be very cryptic I have to say, nothing is straightforward, you are made to work for the answers to your questions!

Whilst on social media, it became apparent that there was a very different view to what we were being told. I started seeing posts from people about these views.

You can maybe gather I was a bit behind in discovering the link here and what the spirit world was trying to tell me in the beginning, and who I needed to be looking for!

It wasn't until I was talking to a friend on messenger, through a social media giant and discussing the world situation, that a well-known conspiracy theorist was mentioned, and suddenly it clicked that the man from my 13th March dream and 17th April experience was the same person, and that was David Icke.

I said to my friend whom I was talking to 'I wonder where he lives and got the reply 'who' I replied 'David Icke' and he told me he lived on the Isle of Wight.

I instantly wondered how far this was from me, so I loaded Google Maps and did a route from my home to the Isle of Wight; the mileage was 251 miles, going back to the dream of visiting this person I had told my husband he lived 250 miles away. To my mind, this was convincing that I was on the right tracks. I considered that proof that somehow, I was meant to know about Mr Icke. I am not sure if that is factually correct, but close enough for me to see the connection.

I then began seeing an advert for the 'Rose/Icke' interview. Brian Rose for London Real was going to be interviewing David Icke on his show, the subject being the pandemic.

It wasn't just one interview though and the first one was held five days after my dream, but I missed that one and the second one initially as I didn't know at the time that this person was David Icke.

These are the dates of all the interviews between Brian Rose and David Icke;

I – The Truth behind the Coronavirus Pandemic, Covid-19 Lockdown and the Economic Crash aired on the 18th March 2020

II – The Coronavirus Conspiracy aired on the 6th April 2020

III – 1,336,138, The Largest Live Stream Conversation Audience in History aired the 3rd May 2020

IV – We Will Not Be Silenced aired on the 14th June 2020

V –The Answer aired on the 2nd August 2020

Referring back to my dream of the two men in the air with silver cords attached holding swords and they were trying to prevent the two men on the ground from cutting them down, I believe this refers to Brian Rose and David Icke been removed from Facebook and YouTube before

Rose/Icke III been aired. This interview had over a million viewers, and yes, I did watch it.

Who is David Icke you might ask? Some of you will know him, and others may not, he is a well-known English conspiracy theorist, a former footballer and sports broadcaster. He has written over twenty books and spoken in over twenty-five countries.

He visited a psychic who told him he was on the earth for a purpose and that he would receive messages from the spirit world. He has been ridiculed because of his beliefs.

Today though many of his predictions have come to fruition.

He also has a quote as follows 'Know the outcome and you see the journey'

I would say to anyone and everyone that reads this book, to do your own research about subjects because how will you ever learn if you don't.

The spirit world led me to David Icke, he wasn't someone I followed, and I had never read any of his books, I knew the minimal regarding what he was about. Yet the spirit world put him into my world, so there must be a reason for them to do that, to learn, to be taught by him.

I trust one hundred percent

11th May 2020

I was watching a series called 'Killing Eve' and was amazed to hear David Icke's name mentioned. Amazed because the series is pre-recorded, it was ironic that it appeared at the time I was receiving information about David.

I did watch via the BBC i-player website, the episode was episode 5, which aired on 20/05/2020

15th July 2020

Upon going to bed I knew there was a lot of energy around, when the light was turned off it became much clearer. Whether I had my eyes open or closed did not matter it was still visible. I know from this experience that my purpose is to try and help people. I have always worked in a service industry, so I understand this. I saw several things, gold spots, small blue squares that were in the distance. Images that floated past me, eyes and more things that wasn't distinguishable, but I knew I was amongst others.

The most recent experience was in **June 2021**, there was going to be a Freedom March in London, and there had been several since the pandemic started but I hadn't felt the urge to attend with living a fair distance away. Sometimes though fate intervenes, and I dreamt about attending a march, I went on my own without my husband, I knew it was something I had to do. About three days later a friend connection messaged me and said she had a spare seat if I'd like to go. Immediately I said yes. One week before it was due to happen, we had a lot of energy, I sensed this energy very close to me. I passed the thought that I would wear my purple hat. The energy dissipated. Yet every night that week we felt this energy.

Friday night arrived and my husband was a little worried about me going, but when I explained that I knew I needed to go as something was going to happen, and wear the colour purple was significant, he realised I needed to go.

Saturday morning, I was awake early and travelled to another town to catch my lift. We arrived in London about

11.30am and made our way to Marble Arch where the march was starting from. The atmosphere was so very positive, smiles, laughter and love shone from everyone. There was no fear. We started to move and walked with purpose. I would say we were about halfway round, and suddenly I heard some noise clapping and shouts. There in front of me was David Icke. I suddenly knew this was why I was meant to be there. There were other people asking for a photo, and I knew I wanted one, I tapped him on his arm and asked if I could have one and he thank fully obliged. I have no doubt this was supposed to happen. My only regret was I didn't get to chat. Putting this into context it was estimated there was around 2 million people at this event. For me to come across him was not a coincidence.

I text my husband to tell him...his words 'Oh did you really? That's brilliant'

Chapter Five

It Doesn't Stop

25th June 2019

This well-known lady has visited me twice in dreams, in this one though I was trying to get somewhere with another couple of people. A taxi appeared out of a nowhere with a lady stood next to it, she said to me 'get in this taxi, but don't take the back seat otherwise the driver will charge you' so I jumped into the front seat.

It felt like she was giving me a helping hand.

The lady was Cilla Black, she had predicted before she died of somebody seeing her own ghost in the future.

23 October 2019

I was attending a course and was in a café with another course attendee buying some of my favourite lemon cheesecake. I then saw a plane in the sky going upwards. But from out of the plane there were grey sacks been dispatched, one of the sacks split open and I caught one of the smaller bags, they were very similar to prescription bags. They were white with the green cross on them. This had also split, and it had tubes of medication in it!

It seems with this dream, that medication was going to be spread far and wide for something. Could it be that I was been shown that medication in the form an injection would be worldwide? Due to planes crossing the world, makes you think doesn't it!

It didn't feel a positive dream though, our feelings can give us so much verification whether in everyday life or dreams.

Whilst at work on the **23rd March** I discovered that it was likely the business would have to close at some point, I then received confirmation we were to close at noon, I received a visit from one of the bosses who said he was sorry, and they would be in touch. From this, I was entered into the furlough scheme.

Strangely I felt very calm, and happy. I knew that I would be able to concentrate on my own small business where I give readings and sell divination products.

I couldn't give one to one reading due to the lockdown, but my sales picked up in those weeks of lockdown, likely due to people being at home and looking for answers.

I also spent time on social media, and someone who I had watched previously, suddenly appeared in my feed with a free challenge for passive income. I signed up, with no hesitation; I resonated with what she said. After the free challenge I signed up for her signature course and it was one of the best things I have done, it gave me a focus for improving my business. It kept me busy whilst at home, and I was thoroughly enjoying my time being at home.

I also started seeing other articles within my news feed, about coronavirus and related posts from people, at this time I didn't particularly have a view on it, but I wasn't scared. I wasn't fearful of going out either.

My husband and I rarely watch the television in our house, and to be honest, the last time I tried to put it on, it wouldn't work. It is sat on a small table gathering dust! I would see bits of mainstream media news online. I mainly use my trusty laptop for most things, and of course, articles of news appeared on my timeline.

16th April 2020

I woke from a dream which involved two ex-colleagues, they were people that hadn't liked me, as I dozed off back to sleep, I could feel myself moving down a tunnel, when I reached the end, I seemed to be in energy, but I didn't see anything else.

To me the ex-colleagues concerned were negative in their views and personas; it was like they could not see as much as me therefore their perception was inhibited. I think this is prevalent across all societies of people.

Yet there is a need for people to listen to their intuition, it is paramount that we all do this.

18th April 2020

This one was a very strange dream, I was in a cafeteria setting and I saw a woman with big white fluffy slippers on, very expensive ones, and she was stepping on something. I was stood in a queue that started moving so I had to move along with it, which left me unable to see what she was stepping on. I possibly thought was it a kitten but dismissed it as I knew it wasn't correct. A little further on I again saw her, and she was stepping on the head of this living being, it raised itself to its knees and I thought she can't do that! So, I left the queue I was in and hurriedly made my way over and pushed this lady out of the way and went to pick up this living being. I was horrified to discover that this living being was a child that had white fur stuck to their face which I pulled off. I took the child with me for safety.

This dream made me feel very sad, as you can imagine. Child abuse has always been prevalent, all over the world. Yet there seemed to be a lot more focus on events happening in the USA around certain people, which seemed to link across the world.

 Which really makes me nauseous, is that could a pair of shoes be made from human skin, and when I look at my dream this is really the context, a rich woman with these huge fluffy slippers on that was really a child! Horrific isn't it. I don't mention this to scare you, but the need is there to make you aware of how some people in a so called civilised society can treat other people in ways that are unimaginable and get away with it because of the power they hold.

14th May 2020

I was dozing off and discovered a lady in the shadows at that time, I asked her name and she told me 'Genevieve', I did a little research and Saint Genevieve from France came up. Quite an unusual name isn't it. I don't know a great deal about her except she did receive visions and prophecies, one where she persuaded the people to pray instead of fleeing.

It is said she held a 'prayer marathon' that diverted Atilla's Huns away from Paris, which in effect saved the city and a lot of lives.

I thought with this that we are being told we need to pray because bad things are coming, in the form of how certain people want our world to be, and we really do not get a say in it. If we though by living a spiritual life we will raise our frequency which will enable us to think for ourselves in a way that will work for us. It can overcome the negativity; strength comes from the people in their pursuit of freedom.

27th May 2020

In this dream I was sat in an office, I could see two men sat in front of a computer screen, and they had a list of names on a spreadsheet and appeared to be moving figures around between people. I recognised one of the men as he I had met him, but I didn't know the other man. After a few minutes of waiting patiently, the man I knew and said to me 'I'm really sorry to tell you this but we won't be able to afford to keep you on'

The next day I messaged my manager to ask if she knew anything, I was obviously concerned. She couldn't really tell me too much, but she did tell me there was a letter coming out. I received the letter a few days after which said I would have to re-apply for my position. I went through the process but really knew it was already decided. I received my redundancy letter on the 10th August.

16th July 2020

Another dream, I was put into a room that had a glass partition in the centre; I could see there were about six to eight people either side of the partition. We were locked in the rooms. I watched in horror as the people on the other side of the partition seemed to melt before my eyes, I was focused on one man, as he looked at me, his skin seemed to come away, all of his internal body dripped from his bones leaving his skeleton, which collapsed to the ground it then disintegrated into dust, him and the others were gone. At this point I woke up.

This I felt in some ways this is what is to come, people will die, and keep dying and it won't be of their own doing, or naturally. I don't want to say that these people were meant to die, and I would not advocate this in any way... yet it worries me enough that I must talk about it.

It felt like it could be an experiment, to see which people out of the two groups would survive, and I was in the group that did. I have no idea who the other people in my room were, yet I feel we were connected. A thought were the people on the other side of the partition 'vaccinated' people and the people in my side 'unvaccinated' or was it they were not spiritual, and we were, makes you think, doesn't it? Yet either way the outcome is not something that any of us would want, there should not be a division in the world due to beliefs. We are all bound together by something that is bigger than any of us, all it requires is for you to see it.

28th July 2020

I was awoken from this dream where a colleague asked me if I had the 'Geo Lamp' I didn't remember much more from this dream, although I have asked my colleague recently, and I was told he knew someone called 'George Lamp' I still wasn't convinced that it was this, due to the dream changing.

At the time I felt it was something to do with a Geo Storm, something to do with the weather, and it seemed to be in Hawaii, where tests had been done to do with the sky.

When I researched more various things came up, for example chemical trails, which I had heard of and knew it came out of aeroplanes, but I wasn't aware it was spraying that was being done in the skies. I discovered a website about geo engineering which was interesting, again this wasn't something that I had looked into before.

I recall driving to work early one morning and seeing a plane with a trail, it was crossing over other trails.

Someone mentioned to me that a lot of people had seen the same in their own areas.

8th August 2020

I don't remember too much about this dream either, but it was about 'face coverings' some people may say 'face masks and others call them 'nappies'

My husband put his hand on me and asked me if I was alright, I woke and told him that I was fighting against being made to wear one in my dream. It freaked me out, there was the feeling of restriction, and for me it wasn't right, it wasn't a good thing to have to do.

A have a phobia from a dental procedure when I was a child so this makes sense to me.

I came to see that others felt the same, and a lot of people didn't.

Face coverings became mandatory from the 24th July 2020 as per the governments oral speech given on the 14th July 2020. There was the requirement to wear them in public places, shops, gyms (which boggles my mind, how can this be right?) and on transportation too buses and trains, flights too.

For me it's really distressing, to see when people are clearly struggling, I said to some to please don't wear it if it is impacting on your ability to breathe.

31st August 2020

Another dream where I have woken and then drifted off back to sleep.

I was driving to the local town, where the road ran alongside a local wood. I saw a tree had come down across the road., I saw a gap and thought I could get through. Yet I stopped as I thought I could do with some wood for sawdust! Yeah, strange I know! I got out of my car and started to pull this huge tree up the road, and then realised I had nothing to saw it with, I noticed there was also people working there too. I started to take the tree back and asked about having it cut down into smaller pieces. As I was waiting a lorry was coming from the other direction, it didn't see what was happening and it crashed into the tree, very quickly a pile up followed as more vehicles crashed into the lorry. My car was lost in the pile up, I said to someone that I wouldn't be able to get home and that I would have to walk to my daughters. Chaos was everywhere. I saw a couple in a car, the man was conscious, but his wife wasn't and looked asleep. Strangely the whole scene had covers around it and over it. Suddenly the road was clear. Everything was gone and I woke.

This was an odd dream, it gave me the impression that events that can happen can be made to disappear, for whatever reason someone would decide on. We are not in charge of our own destiny; we are governed by external forces.

Chapter Six

The American

26th September 2020

I had this dream after 5.30 am in the morning; I had already awoken and drifted off back to sleep.

I had gone to watch someone give a talk, I'm not sure who it was, I expect he wasn't very important, but it was a 'live' cinema venue, I was there on my own. I was sat in a row of four seats to the left of the stage by myself, the cinema was an old one, reminiscent of the 1930's one I went to a lot as a child in Louth, the seats were made of wood, and upholstered in a yellow coloured velvet, well-worn with years of use, it always had a distinct smell when entering, of times gone by, the energies leaving their legacy as the talk hadn't started yet I was listening to music on my earphones connected to my mobile phone whilst waiting for the talk to start, the merging of old and new is not lost on me.

I noticed this man walking around the venue and hadn't taken too much notice apart from a fleeting thought that he was quite attractive. I then realised he was heading in my direction, I looked around to see if he was going towards another person but as he got closer, he said to me **'you didn't think you were going to get away that easily, did you?'** he then walked into the row behind me leapt over the seats and sat down next to me. At this point, I woke up and never got to see the talk! When I woke, I didn't think I would be able to find out anymore as there was nothing to tell me who he was.

As it happened the next morning I was on my social media and a photograph appeared on my screen, it was the same man from my dream, I recognised him straight away, I clicked on the link which took me to a web page, but it didn't tell me who this man was. I often speak to a colleague about my dreams and sent her the picture to ask if she knew who it was, and she said she thought it was Robert Kennedy! I immediately thought of the president that had been assassinated, but she said no it's Robert Kennedy Junior.

My mind really boggles at some of these dreams, and where they take me.

I quote

"The greatest crisis that America faces today is the chronic disease epidemic in America's children"

Robert F Kennedy, Jr

Another website I would recommend is 'The Children's Health Défense'

I was amazed to see the difference in unvaccinated children and vaccinated children in relation to diseases and illnesses, and how much more prevalent they were in the latter group.

On the 24th of September 2021, two days before the visit from Robert Kennedy, our Uk Prime Minister Boris Johnson said the following to the United Nations.

"There are today people who are still actually anti-science, a whole movement called 'the anti-vaxxers' who refuse to acknowledge the evidence that vaccinations have

eradicated smallpox and who by their prejudices are
endangering the very children they want to protect."

I found this video of our Prime Minister Mr Johnson,
through Robert Kennedy's website.

Although I do think it is slightly unfair to believe that
everyone who questions a 'vaccine' is an anti-vaxxer and
not interested in science.

Yet there are points in my life in relation to vaccines that
are I feel significant. The first was when they were giving
out the measles vaccine, I remember my Mum taking me
to the Doctor's for it to be given to me, I also had a bad
cold at the time, in effect I had a virus and the Dr decided
against giving it to me, and that was that and we went
home. The second incident was when I was a teenager, I
received my Tuberculosis vaccine, I believe now I had an
adverse reaction to it, as it blistered, oozed something,
and became a hole in my arm. I remember going
swimming with school and even though I had a plaster on
my arm, I ended up having to be helped out as I nearly
fainted in the pool. It is still noticeable with an indent in

my arm and a scar in the centre, it is roughly the size of a five pence piece.

I have to say though that science wasn't my strong point at school except for the reproduction module; I got 86% in that one and around 30% in all the others! Maybe I should have become a midwife! I received 10 Merit Marks for my improvement…. maths was never my strong point either, yet English was.

The following excerpt I think sums up what is so wrong in so many ways with how our government operates. It is written by John Stone.

"You might think that if the government wants to encourage acceptance of the new collection of COVID-19 vaccines that they are preparing to unleash on the populace that they would want to reassure people of their concerns about any resulting harm"

You may be already aware of the term 'anti-vaxxer' it has been around a long time but currently has taken on a new life in regard to what some people call a person who is against vaccinations.

Chapter Seven

Up Yours!

28th September 2020

In this dream I saw Russell Brand, he was putting his middle finger up to the world. He is an English comedian, radio host, actor, writer and an activist. He is a spiritual person and wants people to awaken. I never followed his career only knew small amounts of information, yet another person shown to me by spirit.

Upon doing some research the next morning, he had done a 'live' video on social media. This then led me to a podcast that Russell did with his guest Satish Kumar.

Satish Kumar is an advanced elder, he is 84 years of age and has lived a full life, one of his feats was doing a peace walk many years ago this was to protest about nuclear weapons. He is a peace activist. I quote the following;

'Humanity and relationship are more important than profit'

'There needs to be a change in the underlying consciousness'

'Our own personal journey of transformation is unique; it is a lifelong journey'

'Spirituality is not in the books, the temple, not in words, it is in every action you do, all with love'

Satish Kumar, a very wise man indeed, knowledge gained from his own lifelong journey. Think though that I found this podcast due to Russell Brand appearing in my dream, the spiritual world is fascinating in how they don't just give you the information outright, but you must work and search for it.

6th October 2020

After turning out the light in the bedroom, I noticed there was a lot of energy with us, I can see the energy, and I asked my husband if he could see it too, he said 'Yes'

I was told 'it wouldn't be long now, and it would come from the East, and there would be storms and huge waves. The numbers 10 and 11 were mentioned, but I don't know what they relate to. I was also told 'The Book of Ezra' and the 'Code of Ethics'

I was told they come when the weather is bad as it disguises their approach, who they are I wasn't sure.

In the Rainbow Good News Bible, a bestselling bible for children, one was given to my son at school which I still have. I read about Ezra who was a scholar with a thorough knowledge of the law of the Lord. His task was to see how well the law was been obeyed in Jerusalem and Judah. I think what this is really telling the people today is that we must find that place within us that will help you understand where you need to be to overcome the challenges of the time.

I am not here to preach to anyone, yet I feel that we need to connect to something much bigger than some of us are prepared to, you are infinite, and this becomes more understood the more you allow yourself to discover it.

I do remember when I left school I received a pocket bible, and I would read a verse or two at bedtime. My dad walked in once on me praying, and apologised as he backed out of the room.

Again, the overriding feeling is we need to awaken to our deep spirituality that is within all of us, and soon before too much time passes.

Chapter Eight

Mind Control

25th November 2020

Before going to sleep I saw John Lennon's face, I closed my eyes and his face came forward in front of me. I immediately told my husband and said I would have to do some research after work the next day.

When I arrived home the next day and researched him, I knew he had been murdered when I was in my early twenties, I went on to discover that it was on the 8th December 1980, by Mark David Chapman. This was unusual, as the murderer earlier the same day had got an autograph from John Lennon. He then returned later that evening and shot him.

The strange thing was he sat down and started to read a book, that being 'The Catcher in the Rye' by J.D.Salinger.

I became very interested when I came across the MK Ultra – Mind Control Operation; it was linked to John Lennon's murderer.

Mk Ultra was a government program that lasted approximately twenty years from 1953-1973.

From this CIA Director, Richard Helms ordered all pertinent documents about the MK Ultra program to be destroyed! A tad suspicious don't you think? A few years later in 1977, around 20,000 documents relating to Mk Ultra were discovered in a separate building. These were mostly involved with the funding of the program, with very little about the actual activities of the program. This became dependant on participants and victims. It involved psychedelic drugs, death, mind control, interrogation, isolation, hypnosis and sensory deprivation.

There were many experiments and smaller projects carried out and were deemed illegal and inhumane. The two projects called Bluebird and Artichoke are the most well-known. The latter's purpose was to find out if there was a way to control a subject! And to what point could they be made to carry out actions against their will! Could ordinary people be willing assassins?

Chapter Nine

The Cat & Byrd

On the **18th November 2020** before waking, I saw the most beautiful image. I am not sure whether the image was a building; I would liken it to the tallest turret on the Disney Castle in Florida or a similarly shaped spaceship. This was because I saw in the foreground circles of shimmering rainbow colours, which were so bright the light refractions from them spread far and wide. The circles of light overlapped in front of the building, and as I looked to my left the mists of the colours were there.

It is difficult for me to describe the effect this had on me, I just know that I was being shown something that was rare and not often seen. This leads me on to my next dream because for me they are relevant and linked.

26th November 2020

This night I received two names, Richard Byrd came first, and sometime after John Sylvester.

Upon researching I came across Admiral Richard Byrd who was in the United States Navy, what intrigued me was the fact he was part of 'Operation High jump' an exploratory expedition into the Antarctic.

What is interesting about this exploration of the Antarctic is the experience that Admiral Byrd had. He in effect discovered a Lost Earth, which was unlike anything he had seen before.

He talked of tall blond people, and a city that pulsates with shimmering rainbow hues of colour.

Did I see something similar?

30th November 2020

Words from spirit

'Coming soon, the first phase, a break in the outer layer of the earth will allow us to come through to the stratosphere. From there we will be able to move freely around the globe. We are not here to hurt you but to save you.

I was told I would have an important role to play, I'm still not sure what that role is, but I do know I had to write this book.

There would be three levels to us and the reference to L7 quadrant. The only thing I could put this L7 to was either a Liverpool postcode or a map grid reference.

Liverpool was one of the first places to go into 'full lockdown'

18th/19th December 2020

In this dream my husband and I were in a street, the police turned up, and my husband told me to go quickly he was arrested and taken away, so I went down some steps it appeared to be under a bridge and I saw two dark-skinned little girls laid together asleep on a bench. There was a pale skinned lady and a young paler skinned girl with her.

She was just about to leave with the pale girl, and I asked where she was going. She told me she was taking the girl to meet a couple that was going to give her a good home. Yet she was leaving the other two girls by themselves. I was astounded that they would be left alone so I took them with me, as I came out from the underground with these two girls a man across the street shouted to me and said 'I have more baking, but my house is full, what shall I do with it' I replied 'put it in the next house' There seemed to be a lot of houses that were not being lived in. As we passed the window and I looked through, I saw egg custards in the top tray, my favourites!

You must ask yourself the question of why many houses are so vacant. Why is there a shortage of food? Why when you investigate the houses do, they look like time has stopped, as if the occupants have just popped out to the shops? Yet there is a layer of dust that shows no one has been there for some time!

What of the children on the streets hidden underground and if they are the right type of child passed on to other wealthy people? Why are the darker skinned children not wanted or needed!

Why did my husband need to be arrested, was it because they know he protected me and would do anything to do that even if he had to give his life to make it happen? It felt to me that I was someone people turned to, to guide them through, the ones that appeared to still be living, but at what cost was that to them. Everything in their physical reality had changed and the aftermath was so much more different to anything from before.

23rd December 2020

I was travelling in a lorry with two men, we came to a bridge that was blocked off but a man came and moved a cone in front of us so we could cross. A little further along there was a man who knelt, and he didn't move, and the lorry went over him and another man also. The driver stopped and reversed back, and both men got up and walked away. The lorry seemed to lose control and ended up sideways crossways to the bridge, and with that, a piece of machinery was coming down from above heading for the top of the cab. I felt there was no way we would get out alive.

One of the two men who I was in the cab with very passionately said to me 'Claire do not listen to anything they say, they are all liars' I woke up then.

This dream was very much around the time when the lorry drivers were not able to get home for Christmas. The words I heard though were as clear as day, and the man was adamant in his words.

I felt a very deliberate attempt on the lives of these men in the lorry, a set up if you will, anything is possible, isn't it?

Chapter Ten

The Clairvoyant

4th January 2021

I could feel a lot of energy in the bedroom; I received the name, Francine.

5th January 2021

Again, this evening there was a tremendous amount of energy. I received the name, Steiner and Russell, at the time I thought it meant Russell Steiner, but upon searching on the internet, I discovered that Fran Russell (Francine possibly)? Is the acting chief of the Steiner schools. These were introduced by Rudolf Steiner, born 1861 and died in 1925. He was a self-claimed clairvoyant and he wrote several books. One of them is called 'The Philosophy of Freedom' which was published in 1894.

I find the following words of Steiner intriguing to me 'the reality of the spiritual world was as certain to me as that of the physical, I felt that the need however, for a sort of justification for this assumption'

I wonder why he felt the need to justify, because what he was undoubtedly doing was speaking his truth, the ultimate truth of what he believed the spiritual world to be, as do I!

Steiner devoted his life's work to building a complete science of the spirit to which he gave the name Anthroposophy. The science is based on the results of observations and is open to anyone who is prepared to follow the path in this form of development he pioneered.

Upon further research I came across this excerpt from;

Fall of the Spirits of Darkness

Lecture 13

The Fallen Spirits Influence in the World

"It will be the main concern of these spirits of darkness to bring confusion into the rightful elements which are now spreading on earth and need to spread in such a way that the spirits of light can continue to be active in them. They will seek to push these in the wrong direction. I have already spoken of one such wrong direction, which is about as paradoxical as is possible. I have pointed out that while

human bodies will develop in such a way that certain spiritualties can find room in them, the materialistic bent, which will spread more and more under the guidance of the spirits of darkness, will work against this and combat it by physical means. I have told you that the spirits of darkness are going to inspire their human hosts, in whom they will be dwelling, to find a vaccine that will drive all inclination towards spirituality out of people's souls when they are still very young, and this will happen in a roundabout way through the living body. Today, bodies are vaccinated against one thing and another; in future, children will be vaccinated with a substance which it will certainly be possible to produce, and this will make them immune so that they do not develop foolish inclinations connected with spiritual life — 'foolish' here, of course, in the eyes of materialists"

"These, as I said, are the beginnings in the field of literature. The whole trend goes in a direction where a way will finally be found to vaccinate bodies so that these bodies will not allow the inclination towards spiritual ideas to develop and all their lives people will believe only in the physical world they perceive with the senses."

After more research, I discovered that Fran Russell published a statement on the 4th February 2021 titled 'Covid Vaccinations – Advice to Schools'. Within the statement it directed me to another article published on the 12 January 2021, titled

'The Anthroposophic Medicine Statement on Vaccination against Sars-Cov-2'

Efficacy

"High efficacy has been shown for short-term prevention of mild to severe disease for the first mRNA-vaccines (vaccines that work by triggering the production of proteins that train the body's immune system) and a viral vector-based vaccine that have received conditional regulatory approvals. Other vaccines based on different vaccination mechanisms are in development or even used extensively without published scientific data of Phase III clinical studies. Data for high-risk groups are still limited. It is still unclear whether and to what extent the vaccines interrupt or reduce viral transmission - we expect timely research data on this key question for pandemic control as well as further data on efficacy."

And

Safety

"Studies of the two authorized mRNA-vaccines and a viral vector-based vaccine show acceptable safety in short-term follow-up. However, rare, serious side effects cannot be ruled out until very large numbers of people have been vaccinated and followed for a longer time. Also, the detection of non-specific effects - which can be positive or negative - requires longer observation periods. We, therefore, call for sufficiently large long-term studies and anonymized vaccination registers that allow a comparison between populations receiving the different vaccines and non-vaccinated populations. This is all the more important since the mRNA technology used in some SARS-CoV-2 vaccines has not been widely used in humans before."

What this tells me is that there is not yet enough data on the efficacy of the vaccine; you may ask what vaccine efficacy is, it wasn't something I myself was familiar with but it is when a group of people are given a vaccine in a clinical trial it is the percentage reduction of disease within that group. This differs from the effectiveness of the vaccine as that is measured when people in a community are given a vaccine, and it is not a part of a clinical trial.

As we know the flu vaccine is modified every year in line with the different strains, where they try to create a match. I have always thought it would be interesting to know how many people who had received the flu vaccination before the pandemic started, and then went on to contract the coronavirus as it later became known.

It is also mentioned that very few vaccines are not 100% effective but can have high levels of effectiveness.

It gives the 'MMR' vaccine as an example, Measles (97%), Mumps (88%) and Rubella (98%). The annual flu vaccine has 40-60% effectiveness.

When my son received his MMR as a young child, exactly ten days after I was awoken during the night by him fitting in his cot, I was a single mum at the time. I grabbed him out of his cot, he was feverish, and to be honest it was so scary. I banged on the wall to my adjoining neighbour hoping she would hear, luckily, she did and came round, by this time I had stripped him off and was bathing him with tepid water to try and bring his temperature down, he did then stop fitting, his colour returned and he started crying, my friend rang the emergency number and as he had stopped fitting it was around 6 am I think, I was advised to take him down to the doctor's surgery at 8 am as soon as they opened. I went down and the Dr checked him over, and I expressed concerns about whether it could be related to the vaccine? I didn't get a straight answer as to whether it did or didn't.

When I first found out about my pregnancy, I received a book with lots of information, in the section about vaccines, it said that that febrile convulsion could happen around ten days after the vaccine was given. My intuition has always been strong, and I just knew I would not let him have any subsequent ones. The feeling stayed with me until I said no.

Not all children suffer side effects, and I was so grateful that my son was okay, but not all children come through their vaccinations unscathed and are left with damages that affect not only their lives but their families too. I do wonder whether there was any permanent damage to him which is unseen, and that really scares me because of what is happening now.

The children, our future generations need to be safe, to be protected as much as is possible.

Chapter Eleven

Time Travel

8th January 2021

In this dream my husband Paul and I were in our home, I looked out of the window and I saw our fence was down, and there was a lot of rubbish strewn across the ground. We went outside to see what was happening, and there was large sheep loose everywhere. Someone was digging a large hole across the bottom of the road; I went down to see what he was doing.

As soon as I saw the hole, I knew they would find a tunnel and it would lead to a temple. The next thing I was in the temple and there was a pious and a man was stood on it and was preaching to all these people, I recognised some of them as being local to the village I lived in. As I looked from him and to the people surrounding me, they were entranced by him, their faces were glazed, they had on hooded cloaks. Then he started asking them to repeat his words after him. I knew this was wrong and I wasn't affected in the same way as the other people.

I stood at the front and held both my arms out, and I said a different word, I think it began with 'ex' I felt strong, and I felt powerful. I know not why. My third eye was hurting incredibly. I was still talking overriding the voice of the preacher. My words I didn't understand and could have been in a different language.

I then felt my husband put his hand on me, and he whispered in my ear the following 'you have been amazing, you have uncovered what was lost' and I felt that it was needed to be known? I felt myself weaken and fall, collapsing on the floor of the temple. The people stood around watching, and I could hear my husband telling them it is ok she will be fine in a few minutes.

The strange thing was with this experience in that whilst I was in this alternative state, my husband had woken from sleep with the urge to turn over and see if I was alright. He put his arm on my shoulder, and said my name, he slightly shook me. It took me several minutes to return to the here and now, my mind was in this other place, yet I was alternating between the two, I remember whimpering as I came around. For the rest of the day, I felt very lethargic, my energy was low, and the journey had taken a lot out of me.

To my mind this wasn't a dream but time travel, was this into the future? I wonder! I know my husband and I have been connected in previous lives before, as I have seen him as he would have been in a different life that we were together in.

26th January 2021

I had a dream about an office and receiving an email, which didn't make sense. I woke up and heard unintelligible talking in my left ear. The next morning a received an alert on my mobile phone which I thought was strange as the email had gone into my junk folder. It was a notification from Robert Kennedy's Health Defence regarding a press conference that was happening. It was to do with frequencies and how it affects people, specifically children.

Early February 2021

I was awake and received the following and heard; 'Ritual of the Order of the Dark Knights and Salvatore?

This seemed quite random, due to the fact I was awake, it came from around the wardrobe area in our bedroom. When I researched, I came across a couple of things, one being the Batman Movies, as one was called 'Dark Night' and in the film was a character called Salvatore, a power-hungry crime lord, he is involved in organized crime, affray, abduction, kidnapping, conspiracy, attempted murder!

Interestingly DC Comics was launching a new series called 'The Dark Knight' it involved Bruce Wayne travelling to London where he encounters a new villain named Equilibrium. I don't think I have watched all the Batman movies, yet I wonder why they have brought it to London in this new series, and why the villain would be called Equilibrium.

When I looked at the definition of this word it is a state of balance or rest due to the equal action of opposing forces. The equal balance between powers and influences. Mental or Emotional balance from dictionary.com.

I knew that when my balance is off, I would say it's my equilibrium, so what does this mean for our bodies, and how does it apply to real life. Haemoglobin is a small molecule that transports oxygen around our bodies, without this occurring we would die. This is very important for our main organs to work at their optimate levels.

So why would a baddie in a film production be called this? For me we need to be in balance for our bodies to work correctly, doesn't make sense does it. If you watched this programme or your children did, they would associate the word equilibrium as something that is bad, evil maybe. Do we really need that put into ours or their minds?

25th February 2021

I was with a group of people I didn't know, a woman and three men. We were on a country lane and where we were been lured towards a trap, it looked like a large box. Suddenly, a car appeared behind us, and we turned and tried to run but we ended up caught.

I was then in a white room, sat in a chair, there was a man who was questioning me about why I was outside, who I was, where I was from and so on. The man held a clipboard with a form on it, he showed it to me, and it appeared to have different tick boxes against a description of a talk. He said to me 'you won't need to do them all' and he put me down for just one of the talks. They felt like rehabilitation talks.

One of the men who was caught with me was put into a more secure section where he was tagged with a type of belt. We had been there a few days and he could come into our side for a time, and there was a man with dark skin there too, but who was also from the more secure section of the facility. There was an altercation between the two men, and the one I knew his belt tag started to give him pain and he said he had to return, he walked away limping.

I was told I could leave at 11 am, but my talk was at 10.45 am and they lasted more than 15 minutes and were compulsory. I decided that I had to go to the talk otherwise I would be kept in the facility and not allowed to leave. I then woke up from this dream.

This reminded in some ways of a series that was on the tv a few years ago where people that were in hiding were captured and tested. That series was about a Flu Pandemic.

I wonder what is needed to be known from this experience, and if I'm honest it isn't good.

Why was I and others with me caught? We were a group of people that weren't vaccinated it felt.

Why did we need to be assessed? To see how dangerous, we were against a different narrative possibly.

Why the need to control people with pain if their actions were not appropriate? Because the control is the pinnacle of their need.

There is also secure facility's been created I believe already in other countries, how long before they are here?

11 March 2021

A very strong experience of spiritual energy before I went to sleep. I was told the following;

Children of Avalon

When I researched, I found a book called Children of Avalon by S.E Wright, when I had the experience my husband Paul, said to me that it was to do with King Arthur.

I downloaded the book on to my Kindle app and read. The main character finds out she is a time traveller. Her part is to help King Arthur save the kingdom from darkness.

Was I being told here that I was a time traveller? As my earlier experience was very significant, I felt.

Winter Gardens Damascus

I didn't find anything that sits right in relation to these words given, although I feel from what I have read that Damascus is a very spiritual place and to have a connection to nature is something that helps us, mentally, physically and spiritually.

Hornchurch

Both myself and my husband researched Hornchurch in Essex, a borough of London. It has some great history to it, including a Raf Station called Suttons Farm (Wikipedia) I always feel there is a reason for receiving the information. The only thing I found was the next stage planning for a Health Hub in Hornchurch, which was given the go ahead in 2019.

'Today marks the next stage on that journey as public consultation on the plan opens' said Julia Lopez MP (Twitter 31st March 2021)

One of twenty top priority hospitals authorised by the Prime Minister Boris Johnson. It remains to be seen whether this has any bearing on current world events now and in the future.

Chapter Twelve

Excitement

14th July 2021

I knew there was energy close by, which became more apparent when the light was extinguished. Paul could see an arc of light, yet I sensed someone close by, I was told David & Goliath, and was also given the name Henry Clifton.

I discovered the following information on an article by David Rowe.

Henry Clifton Sorbet was born 10th May 1826 and died the 9th March 1908, he was from Sheffield which is well known for its steel making of many years. He was inspired to study science after winning a mathematics prize whilst attending college. He was interested in many things of which Petrology was one. This also extended to meteorites too. He used a microscopy, microscope to me and you...he then developed a spectrum microscope which is a combination of a microscope and direct vision spectroscope, Henry ventured into spectroscopic examination of a wide range of natural pigments, one of these been minute blood samples. This study led to the development in forensic applications or as we know it today Forensic DNA. He became known worldwide for this.

I knew the spirit world must have given me Henry's name for a reason, and I found that he was involved in a famous murder trial of 1871. This was due to his blood forensic applications, unfortunately he had to retract his statement due to his findings not being correct. This is where it got interesting for me because as soon as I went to the absorption spectrum web page I could feel it in my body, my heart started racing, my own energy was dancing, that is the only way I can describe the excitement I felt it was like I was meant to find this information. I was guided to it by spirit, through researching Henry Clifton, even now as I am typing this my fingers flying across the keyboard, I can feel the energy within me starting to gain traction. I don't know why it creates this feeling all I know is it's important.

Where I was led to was encyclopedia.com an article on Fraunhofer Lines.

These are dark absorption lines in the solar spectrum. Imagine having a prism and the sunlight passes through where it becomes separated from its component wavelengths.

Think prisms creating rainbows, but what this does is it becomes a spectrum of light frequencies that are visible. What Fraunhofer did was find dark lines intermingled with the colours. They were colours that were missing from the spectrum. He counted 574 lines which are named after him. In today's world tens of thousands more lines have been discovered by astronomers. The question is why doesn't the sun emit these missing colours? Or if they are emitted what then happens to them because they don't reach the earth.

There are three kinds of spectra as follows from nine planets.com. A spectra is a band of colours.

1, Continuous – all the colours of the wavelengths, nothing is missing.

2, Emission – when atoms are excited, they give off light

3, Absorption - Fraunhofer

Of course, there are scientific reasons for these lines, but what if there was another reason? What if there was something that we couldn't comprehend, or don't want to comprehend.

I feel like spirit are needing to say something, so here goes...

'There is nothing on earth we would enjoy more than seeing you all be happy in the place you call home. You should know this is only your temporary home. There is so much you don't know yet and therefore this woman has been chosen to speak our words, these words written are important. Your home is colour it is light; these missing lines belong to our world but there isn't a way to show you. Remember this woman's vision of a ship landed in circles of colour this is us, this is you. There is not much time we are here for you. '

The words above needed to be written from spirit.

David & Goliath, a story from the bible 1 Samuel 17, about a young man who with his courage and faith of God, was the victor in a duel with Goliath, yet it is not just a story about a fight between a young man and an enemy that is so much larger and stronger than he is. It is also about the conflicts of the ages. The story of how Satan rebelled against God, the confrontation between good and evil, between God and his enemy.

When you look at the events that are going on around the world, there is evil living among us, and the people like myself and so many more can see what is happening. There is a need for us to awaken those in slumber.

August 2021

Before going to sleep I was given the following; Jacob's Ladder

There are a few points to consider about this, the first are the films called Jacob's Ladder, the second in the Bible is the dream that Jacob had, thirdly it directs me to the spiritual meanings, and what people did behind the scenes.

I recently watched the remake of the film which was released in 2019. Why would they release this film again? Shouldn't the original be iconic enough to whether time!

I found the film quite odd, how it flipped from one thing to another, creating such confusion for the main character he didn't or couldn't comprehend what his mind was telling him. I also found it disturbing that a drug was used that hadn't been fully trialled, and given unknowingly to allegedly Jacob and his troop. Again, I am led to mind control as I was in relation to John Lennon. The drug been LSD that caused visions and extreme hallucinations.

The original film was released in 1990, the script written by Bruce Joel Rubin. You can find out more on brucejoelruben.com

Aside from Jacob's Ladder he also wrote the film 'Ghost' which starred Patrick Swayze and Demi Moore, I remember been so intrigued with this film, and watched it several times. The film 'Ghost' won Bruce an Oscar, it should be known that Bruce wanted people to connect with the unseen world of their lives, to be able to touch the inner mystery of who we are inside. He is also a meditation teacher, and by putting his spirituality into his scripts allows a different perspective of what we can achieve for ourselves when we really put our minds to it.

Looking at the alternative aspect of Jacob's Ladder in the bible, it tells the story of Jacob dreaming about a ladder that reached from the earth up into heaven.

On this ladder stood God who spoke to him. What I think this is telling us is that if only we listen, we are all fully able to hear 'god' if only we open our minds enough to allow it

Chapter Thirteen

Spirit Talks

When the time is right you will know that you have to undergo changes within your life that are unlike anything you have felt before. You should not question this as it happens to you for a reason, your purpose is within you and you are required to find it. I will not elaborate you just need to know and trust the power that is within you, it is how you use it that will matter. Granted we don't get it right all the time, but that is part of your learning and you cannot stop because of this.

For humanity to overcome what is such a catastrophe of greed and manipulation you need to keep strong to walk in your shoes fully, there cannot be any half truths. To discover who you are is imperative now! I am here within all if you, I can only help you if you ask of me for help there can be no misunderstanding about who you are!

I will not stand by and let humanity do this to itself, this is why I speak through not only this woman, but many, many others who have a role to play to overcome the jealousy and the corruption of others.

Stand with me, your truth is as powerful as I.

There are many fallacies in this world and you must listen to your heart, not the one that beats in your chest, but the one that is your heart centre created from the love of all that is.

We can win this war that has no place in our future.

Unfortunately, many will die from others greed and power do not let this prevent you doing what you know is right. There will be hardships, do not let this stop you.

Forgive those that have hurt you, love unconditionally especially yourself, kindness to others will give you wisdom and knowledge.

Anomalies in the skies will be seen many shapes, lights will be seen. Flowers will wilt, animals will lay they sense the coming. I will appear to those that can see, I just will not find those that cannot see in anyway, they will not survive.

It is written many moons ago that there will be destruction and it will happen, do not fear if you are reading this as you are showing enough thought freedom to look for answers.

We wait in the side lines, we see everything, before anything can be done there needs to be an alignment of souls this will enable us to come through.

People will look at you differently, do not let that deter you. You have to believe that you do not have a choice if you do not start to see what has been done to each and every one of you. Although the mountains will seem hard to climb, once the summit is reached, you will understand. Trust in your feelings as it gives a good indication of what is right and what is wrong.

There are certain steps I would encourage you to do;

Ask yourself daily what is your purpose today?

Ask yourself weekly the one question you never ask yourself the answer will come!

Ask yourself monthly who can help you discover more?

Your true heart will guide you.

I just want to add to this another dream experience I had in it I was outside on a grassed area, there appeared in the sky, two suns and God in the middle, he opened his arms wide. I was not the only person standing on the grass and as I looked around, people started to drop to the ground, it felt like they wouldn't survive. I remained standing along with a few others.

Is this a prophecy? there are unfulfilled prophecies could this be one of them.

Chapter 14

Undated

In this chapter I am letting you know about some other experiences that I am not sure on the timeframe of them, yet I do think they are relevant.

When Dr Klaus visited me in a dream, he was not alone. There was also a woman with him, I asked who she was to which she replied 'just call me Julie'

Dr Marshall H Klaus (1927-2017), he is well known for his study and research on maternal bonding after birth. He realised that if a baby was removed for instance to go into special care the bonding between the mother and child was not as strong as if the mother had kept the baby with her. We should also remember that babies were at one time taken from their mothers and put in a nursery, which maybe made it easier for the staff but not for the mums. It was concluded that the optimum time for a strong maternal bond was in the first hours after birth. These things could help with breast feeding, child development and could reduce the risk of child abuse.

Is there something to be known from this, will there come a time when babies and children are brought up independently of their parents? The bond once again broken at birth, a scary and worrying thought isn't it. Even in today's world we are seen as caretakers of our children.

A dream I had there were lots of scared children behind wire mesh fencing, I couldn't get in to them, they were all huddled together, I didn't know what to do, so I did the only thing I could and started singing to them and held my hand out to them through the fence. They then disappeared one by one as they came closer. I believe I helped these children cross over to the light. They were not captive anymore.

I saw upon closing my eyes the word Abba which to my mind was the band. A few days later I was driving around and heard on my car radio that Abba were releasing a new album. The first song they released is called 'Don't shut me down' there are words in it that really resonate for me it talks of decoding a dream and also a transformation...to me this speaks of an awakening that changes you inside and you see things differently to what you did before.

Chapter Fifteen

My Thoughts

I hadn't thought of writing a book, but with everything I have experienced I couldn't ignore the signs any longer. From the first message in 2016 up to the present day, all of my experiences have led me on a journey of discovery. Unlike anything I have done before.

The names of people that I have been given living and passed and how they have related to the world situation has left me in no doubt that the truth was not being told. We were been well and truly led up the garden path as they say.

A story was been told, one that has caused a tremendous amount of fear in all of the people that believe the story. Not forgetting people's mental health, loss of businesses, illnesses not treated, and the deaths of so many people, not just from a coronavirus but from suicide, cancelled operations, adverse reactions to vaccinations and so much more.

Think about the people that have been questioning this since the beginning, are they people that do their research, yes!

A lot of them are also very spiritual in nature, from all types of religions. This is because we are all one consciousness. There is no divide between me, you or anyone else there never has been.

That has been created by humanity.

In several of my experience's children have been in them. Where I am helping them, protecting them. Who will look after the children if so, many people were to die? Aren't our children, and their children, and all the generations after that the important part of all this, because without them what do we have. If we stand on the side lines and accept everything we are told, even if we are not sure. What happens to our children then? For myself I couldn't not say anything, I couldn't not try and tell people of my experiences, because awareness can be a wonderful thing, but also in some ways a curse. I am telling my story for my children, my grandchildren, and every single child across the world. Ultimately, they need our help.

We all can choose what we do, but also ask yourself, for how much longer will that be the case, until our choice and our free will are no more.

This is a spiritual war between light and dark perse, yet somewhere in the middle is a balance, it does not do any good to be all of one and none of the other. It just doesn't work.

I will never understand how one person can be more important than another, yes, they can be different in so many ways, due to life experiences but does that make a person better than another? Absolutely not!

I think somewhere in our history lines have become blurred, we each have a path to walk, and that is how we come to discover our own truth, in our own way.

If you feel that you are getting lost in the madness of the world, then stop, breathe and look within. Read, listen, educate your mind about what we as humans are capable of. There isn't a right way or a wrong way, there is just your way! Discovering more about who you are within, will open so much more for you. It really is up to you.

What I would ask you to remember is that the information I have received has come from the spirit world, from outside of my five sense reality.

The future, our future will be pretty bleak if we don't awaken, only by doing this will be rise above the fear, with the knowledge that you do have a purpose whatever that may be and a part to play in bringing this world, our world back to us as the spiritual energetic beings that we are.

The next few chapters are a few articles that I wrote before I even thought about this book. Yet they are relevant.

Chapter 16

Magnitude of a Mile

This is another article I wrote which I think is worthwhile to read.

An interesting title don't you think?

Magnitude is the size of an object, it can be of a large size or it can be about the importance of something, and the Mile is a line segment, a measure of distance, a very long way or a great amount.

Quite straightforward it would seem but yet I see an image of a straight road, an invisible translucent field that retracts and shifts with the pressure of it being touched along the linear lines of the roadsides. The white painted lines act as a central partition, creating two halves, they are striking in their simplicity. Yet I can't help but think they are a distraction for the mind, a pre-cursor to try and distract from the things that are yet to come.

This is very much about a journey an undertaking of learning and it can be as hard or as easy as you make it to be. There is a feeling that everything you do within that space of a mile is a foundation, a basis for you to look really deep within yourself, and to find your journey, your meaning, moving your life forward into its next stage of being.

A Mile can be different lengths, as they have changed with time, and place Do not let this put you off taking this journey though, because what you gain from it will undoubtedly change your life in a way you didn't think was possible. There is no right or wrong way in how you do it or how you get there just as long as you do.

The only criteria I see is that you must start at the beginning, an image of feet, one foot either side of the central white line, and from there the decisions are yours to take.

How do you know it is the beginning? I feel that your life experiences, your highs, your lows will in time bring you to a point where you are looking for more; you need that clarification of something which you know is there but has eluded you in so many ways. The times when you thought you were on a breakthrough and yet nothing happened, the feelings of doubt and insecurities that fell upon you that marred your sense of self-worth preventing you moving forward. A thought in your mind so fleeting yet leaves a lasting impression, and you also know there is an importance to it.

Is there an end?

To my mind there is no end, how can there when we have so much to learn. We are energetic beings and we are not meant to be suppressed by the many things of our world that can do this. We have many layers; the expansion of these is what takes us on that journey as we progress through them, we learn more than we knew before. Never under estimate what you can do!

Now are you ready to begin?

Chapter 17

Room with a View

This is another piece I wrote early one morning.

It never occurred to me when I was younger that I was more than I ever thought I was.

I was always attracted to the unseen things, I always thought I didn't have a vivid imagination but yet my time with the King of the Sea tells me different.

As I sit here at 5.15 am waking up with the title 'Room with a View' in my mind, I am looking out through the window sat at my desk. I look beyond the myriad of coloured strings, a veil through to the other side. I gaze beyond the Willow branches to the homes in the distance, where the slight frost glistens from the rooftops. It whispers of the cold outside. The clear blue unmarked sky above shines bright as the morning sun appears on the other side of our house, yet it is also marred by the upright masts of a neighbour's life of connection by radio to an outside world.

The branches of the Willow sway gently, the new year's growth is young and fresh. The little bird that rests on the wire, shakes and flutters his body, dancing in the morning sun with his daily routine, he then flies off to start his day. My three crystal balls align on the windowsill, and are cold to the touch, appearing misted, and a tool for the unseen worlds. A glimpse into something more that often eludes so many, the ones that have spent time in progressing themselves in the search for their Soul are able to see that which is out of reach.

I love the silence as I sit here whilst people sleep, yet I love to listen to thunder and rain to sleep!

As a woman, a wife, a mother and grandmother my life is where it should be at this moment in time. My learnings are ongoing, and always will be.

It has taken time for me to reach this point.

Where are you right now?

Wherever you are at this moment in time, you are exactly where you need to be, because if you bypass your now you may not be able to reach the place within, the place we attain to find.

Belief is a powerful word, yet having belief you need to have trust that it will happen, and you will get there.

Chapter 18

Aura

The following is some channelled words given about Aura's

"It is quite interesting how one defines something as unique as energy. There are many different ways of how one may understand the purpose of energy and where it resides within the etheric body.

The external pathway that surrounds each and every one of us is unique to that individual.

There should be more understanding of how and why it works

His energy protects, it forms a movable shield, it waves and shimmers when it is breached.

For us to gain the best from it, learn to feel it, to sense it, to investigate it, only then can its full force be analysed gaining more understanding of your own power that you attain from that energy.

I am saying this to you as to know this will help you going forward.

Nothing is set as yet but prepare for changes, raise your vibrational energy.

Thank you

Chapter 19

On the Wings of Love

I came down this morning to open the door to be welcomed by a beautiful sight in the sky, a pair of wings outstretched, gorgeous in their entirety, gliding across the blossoming sky.

A timely reminder of how we must trust and believe in the purity of our origins and that what we experience is as it should be at this point in time. There is much to be said about how we allow ourselves to be challenged and what we learn from those challenges. I talk about the spiritual core that is within us all, the one that should need no introduction but it would seem that a great many have lost this knowledge about themselves. There has been too many decades and layers of physiological damage to the part that resides in us that we can regain if only we would just try, if we don't allow ourselves to keep forgetting and remember. I would urge each and every one of you that can, take some time to really get to know you, dig really deep and what may frighten you when you reach it is part of the process of truly understanding the power we have over our own true self. By overcoming trials and tribulations that have impacted on us and created layer upon layer that seems like a dense fog, will be released and allow your love, your light to once again shine through.

How does this make you feel? Do you feel the beauty of the words? Does it connect to you on a different level? Does it touch your soul?

Chapter Twenty

Movie Nights

I've never been what you would call a movie buff. Yet in some ways I do feel that movies are a way of a message been put out to people so it is in their mind.

Some films that I think are this type, some are from when I was a lot younger...

Logan's Run – What happened to all the older people? Why are people not allowed to live past 30? Interesting they have a life clock put in at birth! Why are they prevented from venturing outside?

Mad Max – A place where people are fierce for their own survival, a lone warrior. Social collapse causes the wastelands. Interestingly, there was no films between 1985 and 2015, and then in 2020 it was announced a new film to be released.

Terminator – Robotic people from the future, trying to prevent change initially. A mother protecting her son from danger. A battle for survival between the human race and a synthetic intelligence.

The Hunger Games – The rich and wealthy get to watch human games of children, which is a nationally televised event.

Level 16 – Where young girls are bought from poor families. Kept in a facility, health checked. With the promise of becoming adopted. That is not what happens, they are chosen but they do not live past level 16.

Total Recall – Espionage on Mars! Is it real though or to do with memory implants?

The Handmaids Tale – A fabricated state where people lose their freedom, many women have become sterile. Women are controlled, used and punished. A fascinating series!

I have an early copy of this book which I read at around eighteen. Yet it took many years to come to our screens, why is that?

Equilibrium – where people take a drug daily to stop them feeling. To feel is punishable by death

These are just a few that I recall, made for out entertainment. Yet where do these ideas come from in the first instance? How can subliminal messages be given to people? It's all in the entertainment.

This is my truth

It's time for you to awaken

Printed in Great Britain
by Amazon

86981907R00078